BLAST RADIUS

BLAST RADIUS

Poems by
Douglas E. Self

Accents Publishing • Lexington, Kentucky • 2024

Printed in the United States of America

Accents Publishing
Editor: Katerina Stoykova
Cover Image by Ananyo C.

Library of Congress Control Number: 2024932078
ISBN: 978-1-961127-06-7
First Edition

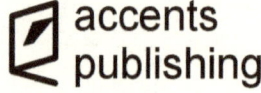

Accents Publishing is an independent press for brilliant voices. For a catalog of current and upcoming titles, please visit us on the Web at

www.accents-publishing.com

CONTENTS

In the past week, how much were you bothered by:

Taking too many risks or doing things that could cause you harm?

FIRST TIME

Most guys tell me they've already figured out how they're gonna kill me,
Said Mr. VA Therapist, as if he were wagging
all of his kid's fancy achievements in my face.
Is that right, I say. Is that right?
Yep.
So why don't you tell me why you're here.
Apparently for nothing at all.
Why do you say that?
Because I only want to kill me

LIGHT DUTY—10 DAYS

A cracked root from a root canal six years prior.
An infection eating through the jawbone.

Army dentists piled around gawking at something they've only
seen in history books, when they didn't have modern dentistry.

Two-hour surgery requiring four days bedrest.

No wearing a helmet for 10 days.
Oxy prescription every 4–6 hours as needed for pain.

Yum.

COPING

Sweaty forehead. Empty-stomach-except-for-Percocet &
beerpangs almost double me over on the bar stool.

Order another bottle of Miller Lite and a
shot of Black Haus.

Friends and I sat around watching videos of people
beating the shit out of each other before coming to the bar.

I want to fight right now but the energy humming through me—
I won't break it. I can't.

I'm on my way to oblivion,
but I'm not there yet.

Dirty-blonde walks by, she's checking you out hard,
What are you gonna do about that?

Nothing. Absolutely nothing.
I'm not here for that tonight.

Stomach lining screams, bending me in a figurative half
because I must maintain composure.

Another bottle of beer and another
shot, followed by claps on the back.

It's good to see you, brother.
Don't worry about it. I got this round.

Now c'mon let's go out back and smoke this thing up.
Yeah sure, I'll be right back. I just gotta piss.

Man, we're glad you're home.
Safe and sound.

Thanks. Now hand me my beer—
I need to wash another pill down.

PRE-IRAQ TRAINING MINDSET

Bang, bang, shoot bad guy.
Drive truck.
Don't blow up.
Man, it's freezing out here.
When is final formation?
Hey, you think we'll have time to get some beers
and go to the strip club?

SACRIFICE

Pay fifty bucks,
she walks up,
your buddy thinks
he's gonna—

Stuck on stage,
shirtless and cuffed—to a chair,
she's using his belt. Snap.
Damn—check out those welts.

And this is what some soldiers
did after a day of pre-war training;
black eyes and bloody lips
patriotically delivered by strippers working for tips.

In the past week, how much were you bothered by:

Repeated, disturbing dreams of the stressful experience?

EXPLOSIONS ARE MY DREAMS

The conviviality I strive for because
I live lamenting the next breath
that lies in wait for me to scream—

Out, in and out, the efficiency of the power plant
that is my body denies my attempts
at suffocation.

I cannot wait to sleep
to forget about waking up.
Up the blast radius blows up

in a ring of Earthly debris and death.
Raising me above all.
The glorious goodnight.

In the past week, how much were you bothered by:

Trouble falling or staying asleep?

IN BETWEEN TWO THIGHS

A right hand
slaps the side of my
passed-out-face-down head.
You're asleep! Really? While going down on me?!
I'm going all the time. Can't stop moving.

Sleep man, sleep is different over there—
in the box.

The time zone difference is breaking me.

No.   No.
I was, I was just taking a break.

Sleep man, sleep is different over here.
But she doesn't care.   Doesn't know.
Our time will blow away.
Like the sounds of sleep,
man, sleep.

In the past week, how much were you bothered by:

Blaming yourself or someone else for the stressful experience or what happened after it?

I WONDERED WHAT IT WOULD BE LIKE TO KILL

To hover over their body.

Grimly,

with such power

and magnificence.

Adore me.

Because I am your life now.

WHY HAVEN'T YOU FILED FOR VA DISABILITY YET?

Why should I? I mean no one made me join. And besides I hear these fucking guys at reserve duty coaching each other up about what to say if they have PTSD. If their back is hurting. Or if they're having nightmares.

Well, I have nightmares, Doc.
Explosions. Even if the dream is about Disneyland.
Mickey or one of his cronies is gonna get it.
They'll find the I.E.D. and when they do—
It won't be Mickey's face anymore, Doc.
It will be mine.
Or someone I served with in Iraq.
That's awful, but it still doesn't explain why you haven't filed for
    disability.
It's clear you don't need any coaching and that you're not lying.
What's really keeping you from filing that claim?

Because, Doc.
Because what?
Because filing that claim means I accept it.

Accept what? Weakness.

PROFITEERS

I honestly never saw the enemy in Iraq.

Not once.

I saw Halliburton a lot though.

INTERNAL PUSHBACK

You don't know shit about PTSD. Stop using it as an excuse for your misery. PTSD is a myth made up by doctors in an attempt to rid of us of the culpability of voluntarily signing the contract. Of voluntarily wanting to take up the rifle. Of gladly needing to experience war. The thrill, the kill, and the frills. No one pointed a gun at my head to serve. I needed a master. And, in turn, I wanted to be the master pointing the gun at whomever they identified as the enemy. I wanted to kill. I wanted to die. In combat. With honor.

Like a pussy, I came home. With nothing but complaints and a big fat zero for a combat body count.

In the past week, how much were you bothered by:

*Repeated, disturbing, and unwanted memories
of the stressful experience?*

I.E.D.

I sucked death's tongue,
bit down on her lips,
pulled her head down firm,
exposing her neck.

Her smile grew wide
as she knelt down
just to take me in
and spit me out.

BUT WE ARE ALIVE

A puppy
crosses the road.

An up-armored vehicle
believes this to be an enemy ruse.

To slow it down.
To blow it up.

Man, I know they trained to us to keep going.
But are you really going to—

Damn, dude.
You're cold hearted.

0200-0600 TOWER GUARD SHIFT DURING A MORTAR ATTACK THAT WAKES YOUR PARTNER UP

Oh shit. Call that in, man.

Huh, what?

You've got the radio. I'm getting the azimuth. Call it in.

Call what in?

Oh, I don't know maybe that explosion 200 yards in front of us.

What? No, I don't see anything.

What do you mean you don't see anything. Oh, fuck me. Would you put your glasses on?

THE WAITING GAME

Four hours now. We've been sitting in the same spot on
    MSR[1] Tampa—
Four hours now. It's 125 degrees outside.
Probably close to 150 in the cab of this up-armored vehicle.
We've been sitting here for hours now—
I could have sworn it was four days,
but it's not.

Four hours and still awaiting the arrival of E.O.D.[2] to investigate that
suspicious pile of stacked rocks on the side of the road.
Honestly—I wish people would stop calling in possible IEDs.
Just let them blow. It's more efficient for logistical flow.

---

1.   MSR = Main Supply Route or, in laymen's terms: A military road name.
2.   EOD = Explosives Ordinance Disposal

In the past week, how much were you bothered by:

Loss of interest in activities that you used to enjoy?

MY FAVORITE THINGS:

Sitting at work doing nothing (almost a sexual pleasure).
Sitting at home doing nothing (wishing I was at work doing
nothing).

An unpleasantness arrives:

Listening to the wife tell me all the things that I don't do right.
Are you really gonna eat that? You never wanna have sex. Why
are you making that sandwich that way? Wouldn't it make more
sense to do it my way? You won't talk to me. What do you mean
I always tell you what you're doing wrong? I'm sorry you feel
that way ...

What she doesn't realize is that:

My eyelids must be armored because they are too heavy to lift in
the morning, and that my side of the bed is a quicksand lover
because I never want to get up.

For tomorrow is here, today.
Excruciatingly, here.
Waiting for me as if I were prey.

WHAT HAVE I BECOME?

I am molasses,
paralyzed.

COMBAT VETERANS IN HIDING

Sparklers, spinners, wheels, smoke, firecrackers, Roman candles, rockets, cakes, fountains, and artillery shells.

Blasts, bursts, detonations, bangs, blowouts, claps, cracks, percussion, and pops.

Accompanied by the oohs and the ahs of the American public who love to say: "Thank you for your service but this a free country, and it's our constitutional right to blow shit up today."

From under a bed in a darkened room I scream,

Fuck you Fourth of July!

That's right. I said it.

Go straight—to hell.

In the past week, how much were you bothered by:

Feeling distant or cut off from other people?

DUAL DIAGNOSIS

They say I'm different.
That I'm always drunk.
They don't understand.

I want to leave.
I want go home.
Back to Iraq.

Where PTSD
doesn't show.

In the past week, how much were you bothered by:

Trouble experiencing positive feelings (for example, being unable to feel happiness or have loving feelings for people close to you)?

PUSHED YOU AWAY

One plus one equals two;
The simplest arithmetic
frightens me.

OF AN ATOM

While listening to her husband
Confess to fucking the nucleus

While listening to her husband
During the fall

Of her marriage
During the fall

She sits silently
Seeking a single free neutron

For position
Seeking a single free neutron

Showing a smile
Over the Earth like a Lunar Eclipse

Showing a smile
In the midst of a cosmic battle

       And that matters
        During the fall
        During the silence
        During the confession
        Of his love for
        Radioactive material

TILL DEATH DO US PART

Ten thousand car alarms sound
the drop of the judge's pen on
the dissolution of marriage.

All you have to do now is—
believe it.

In the past week, how much were you bothered by:

Thoughts that you would be better off dead,
or of hurting yourself in some way?

A GOOD IDEATION

That Kurt Cobain was onto something:

You only need to apply a little pressure—
To relieve a lot …

Epilogue

NOT MY FINAL MESSAGE

Garbage on the side of the road will explode. Everyone in the grocery store is a threat. Your children unsuspectedly jumping on your back is a calculated attack. It only takes someone to disagree with you over the simplest thing for you to lose your shit. Your family walks on eggshells, and you know it.

On a daily basis, ending it all isn't such a bad idea. Besides, you think your absence is better for everyone.

But you can't. You won't. For some reason that eludes you now, you just won't.

Your children need a father or a mother. Your family needs a son or a daughter or a sister or brother. Your friends need a friend. And you need a you.

Other Vets tell you the VA is full of shit and incompetent, but deep down you know better.

There is … You have, hope. Of a different life. A life where you don't believe your trauma makes you interesting. A life where you don't feel like a corpse every day.

A life, dare you say, that might inspire.

It starts with one step.

An email or phone call saying:

You're ready.

You need help.

Then show up.

No matter how uncomfortable it is. No matter how much it hurts. No matter how much you try to convince yourself that "it's really not that bad," or "what's the use anyhow?"

Never stop—

showing up.

ACKNOWLEDGMENTS

I'd like to thank the Lexington, Kentucky VA hospital, especially Dr. Domino & Dr. Johnson: I'm breathing today because of the work we did together.

To my mom, dad, step-dad, sisters, children, and friends: Thank you for putting up with me all of these years.

To all of the active service members and military veterans: You're not alone. You're not the first to feel this way. Reach out. There are hands waiting to connect.

ABOUT THE AUTHOR

Douglas Self is a father, a poet, and a USMC, U.S. Army Reserve, and Iraq War Veteran who resides in Lexington, Kentucky. He has a bachelor's degree in English & Creative Writing from Southern New Hampshire University, and an audio / video engineering trade school certificate from the Lexington School for the Recording Arts. His hope for this collection is that it inspires other military / combat veterans to seek help.

www.ingramcontent.com/pod-product-compliance
Lightning Source LLC
Chambersburg PA
CBHW031239120626
46545CB00003B/1186